HAUS CURIOSITIES

A Love Affair with Europe

About the Author

Giles Radice has been in parliament for 46 years, 28 of them in the Commons and 18 in the Lords. He chaired the influential Commons Treasury Committee and the European subcommittee of Economic and Monetary Affairs in the Lords. He also served as Chair of the Franco-British Council, the European Movement, the British Association for Central and Eastern Europe, and Policy Network, the international think tank. He is the recipient of the Order of Merit of the Federal Republic of Germany and the French Legion of Honour.

As a writer and historian, he is the author of 15 books, including *Offshore: Britain and the European Idea*; *The New Germans*; *Friends and Rivals: Crosland, Jenkins and Healey*; and *Odd Couples: The Great Political Pairings of Modern Britain*.

Giles Radice

A LOVE AFFAIR WITH EUROPE

The Case for a European Future

HAUS
CURIOSITIES

First published in 2019 by
Haus Publishing
4 Cinnamon Row
London SW11 3TW

A CIP catalogue record for this book is
available from the British Library

ISBN: 978-1-910376-99-7
eISBN: 978-1-912208-15-9

Typeset in Garamond by MacGuru Ltd

Printed in Czech Republic

www.hauspublishing.com

To Lisanne, and all my family, especially
my children and grandchildren

Contents

Acknowledgements

This booklet, which is by way of an *Apologia Pro Vita Sua*, has benefitted from the wise advice of others.

My wife, Lisanne Radice, my brother, Jonathan Radice, and my daughter Sophie Radice, have all read various drafts, as have Andrew Blick, Penny Bochum, Dianne Hayter, Peter Hennessy and Peter Liddle. I have also profited from conversations with Andrew Adonis, Brian Crowe, Quentin Davies, Charles Falconer, Rachel Farrow-Smith, Charles Grant, Bruce Grocott, John Horam, Brian and Anne Lapping, David Lea, John Monks, George Robertson, Christopher Tugendhat, William Wallace and Larry Whitty.

I would also like to thank Harry Hall for his meticulous editorial assistance and advice, and his team at Haus Publishing.

Introduction

As a supporter of European unity since the age of 18, I was shattered by the victory of the Leave campaign in the June 2016 referendum on the United Kingdom's membership of the European Union (EU).

My wife and I had worked hard for the Remain campaign in Lincoln in the weeks before referendum day, and although we met a growing number of Leave supporters during our door-to-door campaigns, we still hoped for a Remain victory. However, when the early results came in from the north of England (with a big win for the Leavers in Sunderland and with the Remainers only just ahead in Newcastle), we realised that the odds were now against a favourable outcome. The final result confirmed our worst fears: 52 per cent for Leave and 48 per cent for Remain.

I was devastated by the Leave win. As well as a personal defeat, I saw it as a disaster for both the UK and Europe. Michael Bloomberg, the American media mogul, expressed my thoughts exactly when he said, "it was the stupidest thing any country has ever done." And what made the Remain defeat even harder to bear was the reaction of my grandchildren. One of them, with tears in his eyes and in words I shall never forget, cried out, "Grandpa, you do realise that your generation has just ruined my life!"

Like many of my colleagues on the Remain side, I was

shocked and uncertain about what should be done next. But my friend Peter Hennessy came to my rescue by suggesting that I write a short account of how I became a supporter both of the EU and of the UK's membership of it.

In this book, I also describe the way in which, following the 1975 referendum, Europe became my main concern within the Labour Party and in parliament; why – despite over 40 years of membership – the British remained reluctant Europeans, culminating in the narrow victory for the Leave campaign in the 2016 referendum; and why Brexit could yet be prevented from becoming a self-inflicted wound.

In the three years since the referendum, it has become ever more certain that leaving the EU – especially at such a dangerous time for the West – is an unacceptably high-risk strategy that could lead to disaster for the UK. In contrast, the case for remaining in the EU is gathering force by the day. As I write, it is becoming increasingly clear to me that, even if we did leave the EU at the end of the Article 50 period (which is still by no means certain), the UK will decide to rejoin sooner or later. The last section sets out the reasoning behind my thinking, and so this short book – which started as a requiem – ends on a more optimistic note.

A Patriot for Europe

Although I shall always be a committed European, I am also a British patriot. I was brought up on the exploits of Drake, Wolfe, Nelson and Wellington, and as a child, I was taught to admire the contribution of my forebears to this country. Members of my father's family, which is of Italian descent, have been British civil servants, academics, teachers and business executives. On my mother's side, I come from a long line of Lincolnshire MPs, justices of the peace (JPs), soldiers and farmers. My relations on both my father's and mother's sides fought – and died – for Britain, and I myself am proud to have served as a national service ensign in the Coldstream Guards.

Above all, I value Britain's contribution to world civilisation, especially its scientific and technological achievements; its magnificent language and literature; its development of parliamentary democracy and the formation of trade unions; and its commitment to the rule of law, a non-partisan civil service and the creation of the welfare state.

I can therefore understand, if not sympathise with, those who find it difficult to accept that Britain is now no more (and no less) than a medium-sized European power. Even during my own lifetime, I have seen a dramatic shift. When I was in India as a child during the last days of the British Raj, I used to gaze at the map of the world, a quarter of which was coloured in red for the British Empire. Now, in the 21st century, we have once again become a small but relatively prosperous group of offshore islands, linked by a tunnel to the European mainland. It is this momentous change of circumstance that makes it inevitable that, whether as part of the EU or not, Britain's future lies with its neighbours on the continent.

Throughout my teenage years, my interest in continental Europe grew. France, which the Elizabethan poet and courtier Sir Philip Sidney called "that sweet enemy", was only a few miles away across the Channel, and I spent many happy holidays on the windswept beaches of Brittany. Later, I was enchanted by the intense light of Provence and by the stunning blue of the Cote d'Azur. And staying with a Parisian family at the age of 16, I fell in love for life with France's wonderful capital.

On the other side of the Alps lay Italy, quite literally the 'land of my fathers'. My great-great-grandfather Evasio was a radical patriot, fortunate enough to escape a death sentence following the abortive 1821 uprisings in Italy by emigrating to Britain. He returned in 1848 (the year of revolutions throughout Europe) to Turin, where – though by then a British subject – he became an MP in the first democratic parliament on the Italian Peninsula and was, for a few months, its representative to the Frankfurt Parliament of Professors. Tracing his footsteps, I saw a facsimile of his 1821 death sentence in Turin's National Museum of the Italian Risorgimento and also paid a visit to Vercelli, Evasio's former constituency.

Having spent a few months in Tuscany in the 1920s, my father told me that I must see the region. He was right. In many ways, Tuscany has the classic Italian landscape, with its enchanting hill towns and red-roofed farmhouses surrounded by vineyards and olive groves and framed by pencil-thin cypress trees. I was similarly bowled over by the Italian cities, especially the Renaissance glories of Florence, the watery magic of Venice and, of course, the Eternal City of Rome, with a history stretching back 28 centuries and with more fine buildings and monuments than anywhere else in the world.

By my early twenties, I had imbibed the basics of European culture almost by a process of osmosis. In terms of art, my early favourites were the 'Winged Victory of Samothrace' soaring triumphantly at the top of the Daru Staircase in the Louvre, Sandro Botticelli's masterpiece 'The Birth of Venus' in Florence's Uffizi Gallery and Pablo Picasso's enigmatic 'Girl in a Chemise' in London's Tate Gallery.

My taste in music was orthodox, shaped by the three German greats: Bach, Mozart and Beethoven. But I also admired Stravinsky, especially the pulsating rhythms of 'The Rite of Spring'. Jazz is, of course, an Afro-American creation, but I first heard the marvellous saxophonist Sidney Bechet in Paris, then a centre of European jazz.

Meanwhile, the cinema on Walton Street in Oxford introduced me to the exciting post-war European film scene. There, I saw Vittorio De Sica's 'Bicycle Thieves' and Federico Fellini's 'La Strada', as well as some of the stylish productions of the French nouvelle vague, like Alain Resnais' 'Hiroshima Mon Amour' and 'Last Year at Marienbad'. I loved Ingmar Bergman's wonderful films, especially the enchanting 'Wild Strawberries' and the disturbing 'The Seventh Seal'.

However, it was probably my eclectic reading of continental literature that provided the firmest base for my European education. At school, I picked up a smattering of the Greek and

Latin classics and was enthralled by Homer's epic poems *The Iliad* and *The Odyssey*, which are still beside my bed today. But, in what is perhaps an indication of my future direction, I was most impressed by the Greek and Roman historians, above all by Thucydides and his *History of the Peloponnesian War*. For the first time in historical literature, Thucydides aimed to be objective and based his account on oral and written evidence.

Later, I dipped into the works of the French writers of the Renaissance and the Enlightenment. Montaigne was (and still is) my favourite. With his humanity and curiosity about life, he is arguably the first modern writer, more relevant for all his realism than the Italian Machiavelli. As the French novelist Flaubert advised a friend, "read him in order to live."

Of the French 19th- and early-20th-century novelists, it was Stendhal – whose *Le Rouge et Le Noir* and *La Chartreuse de Parme* display his mastery of characterisation and his fascination with human psychology – who passed my bedside test. For me, Stendhal is up there with the Russian grandmasters of literature.

Travelling to the United States for holidays, seminars and conferences, I also made an important discovery. Despite our common language, America felt more foreign to me than many countries of continental Europe. I missed the familiar European reference points – the old cities and towns, medieval churches and cathedrals, the long-settled landscape.

Looking out from the top of my south-Lincolnshire hill, for example, I can count six parish churches and one great cathedral. If I were on a Bavarian, Burgundian or Umbrian hill, I would almost certainly be able to spot a similar number of ecclesiastical buildings which, if somewhat different in style, would recognisably belong to the same Christian civilization. Heading north and crossing the Tyne at Newcastle, you can see a magnificent Plantagenet castle built by Henry II. Similar castles can be found not only throughout the British Isles, but also in northern and western France, either built or restored by Henry II, whose energy, according to the medieval chronicler Walter Map, disturbed almost half of Christendom. This is a reminder that, in the 12th century, England belonged to the powerful Angevin Empire which stretched far beyond the Channel to the south-west of France.

Indeed, from the earliest times, the British Isles have shared a common experience with the continent, including the Megalithic era; the Celtic period; the legacy of the Roman Empire; the pervasive influence of Christian Europe; the Renaissance; the European Enlightenment of the late 17th and 18th centuries; the Industrial Revolution, of which Britain was the pioneer; and the imperial expansion of which Britain was, again, the leading exponent. Voltaire expressed the impact of this beautifully when he said that "the peoples of Europe share humane principles which are not found in other parts of the world. Christian Europeans are as the ancient Greeks used to be: they may go to war with each other, but despite these conflicts they do observe the proprieties [so] that a Frenchman and an Englishman and a German, when they meet, often seem as if they were born in the same town."

The catastrophic wars of the 20th century affected nearly all of Europe. Just inside my grandfather's front door was a brass shell case, which he used as a doorstop. It was a disturbing memento brought back from the war of 1914–18. Like millions of Britons, he had crossed the Channel to fight in

Flanders and northern France. Two decades later, his son was an officer in the Allied army, which landed in Normandy, liberated France and, with the Red Army, defeated Hitler.

Involvement in two European wars should have been enough to remind the British that their fate was inextricably linked to the European continent. Yet because they were on the winning side and still considered the UK to be a world power, they believed that they could stand aloof from the first proposals for an EU put forward by the defeated countries of mainland Europe.

My 'road to Damascus' moment happened around this time. It was in summer 1955, ten years after the end of the Second World War, between leaving school and starting national service, that I, somewhat ambitiously, set out to cycle from Rotterdam to Rome. As the foreign ministers of the six founding member states (France, Germany, Italy, the Netherlands, Belgium and Luxembourg) prepared for the Messina conference, which would lay the foundations for the Common Market, I peddled along the roads of northern Europe. Most nights, I stayed at youth hostels, where I met my continental contemporaries. Excitedly, we discussed the idea of building a new and better Europe in which war – whose detritus still visibly scarred the land – would be banished forever and prosperity assured for all. As we talked, it became clear to me not only that it was right for my fellow Europeans to unite, but that Britain must not divorce itself from such a bold and constructive project. Britain had to join the budding EU.

I was deeply disappointed that British politicians, who with their imperialist mentality were still insistent on behaving like leaders of a world power, refused to participate in the creation of the European Common Market. In the early 1950s, both the Attlee and Churchill governments rejected the opportunity to join the European Coal and Steel Community. When, in 1955, Britain was invited to become a founder member of the Common Market, the invitation was turned down. It was symptomatic of the British government's attitude that, while the six founders were represented at the crucial Messina conference by their foreign ministers, Britain was not there at all. And in the successful negotiations that followed, Britain sent only a middle-ranking Board of Trade civil servant, Russell Brotherton, as an observer. Anthony Eden, who succeeded Churchill as Prime Minister, was far more concerned with Britain's relationship with the United States and the link with the Commonwealth. Commenting on closer integration with Europe, he said: "We know in our bones we cannot do it."

Britain's failure to understand the significance of what was happening on the continent cost the country dearly. There is little doubt that, if Britain had been involved in the European Community (EC) from the beginning, its rules – particularly as regards agriculture – would have been far more favourable to British interests. The British could also have achieved a better deal for the Commonwealth. But due to their lack of foresight and vision, successive British governments missed the opportunity to create an EC at least partly in their own image.

Nevertheless, the argument for British membership still remained strong on political as well as economic grounds. As the former American Secretary of State Dean Acheson said in 1962, "Great Britain has lost an empire and has not yet found a role." My personal support for British membership was reinforced by a trip to the German Federal Republic. In the summer of 1962, I travelled to Berlin to attend the first Anglo-German Young Königswinter Conference, a junior version of the annual conference which brought together British and German post-war leaders to debate common problems. A few months previously, the Berlin Wall had been erected by the East German regime, not so much to keep others out, but to keep its own people in. With my fellow participants (including the ebullient John Smith, future leader of the British Labour Party), I crossed into East Berlin at Checkpoint Charlie. Being in East Berlin, even for a few hours, was a deeply depressing experience. Apart from a few pompous Stalinist official buildings, the city was crumbling and grey. You could almost smell the hopelessness and despair of its inhabitants who scuttled by with their heads bowed. We were all relieved to return to the bright lights and bustle of West Berlin, which was very much a showcase for the new Federal Republic.

As my plane took off from West Berlin's Tempelhof Airport, I reflected on this memorable experience. Our visit to East Berlin had reminded me that, although it was behind the Iron Curtain, its fate – as well as that of the rest of eastern Europe – was our concern.

I was also very much impressed by the remarkable recovery of the Federal Republic. From the Stunde Null (or Zero Hour) of its devastating defeat, West Germany had risen from the ruins. The democratic Federal Republic had been established in 1949, the Allied occupation had been ended and the Federal Republic had become a founder member of the EC and a member of NATO. Boosted by its access to the markets of western Europe, the German economy was beginning to overtake that of the UK. Indeed, there was a growing danger that we would be left behind. To my mind, the case for British entry was greatly strengthened by this example of the success of the Federal Republic inside the EC.

Fortunately, leading British politicians were at last beginning to wake up to the increasing power and influence of the EC. In 1960, the British Prime Minister, Harold Macmillan, asked the Permanent Secretary of the Treasury to carry out an investigation into the advantages and disadvantages of the UK's membership of the EC. The report concluded that the existing members of the EC "may become a bloc comparable in influence with the United States and USSR, and if that happens and if we remain outside, our relative position in the world is bound to decline." A year later, Macmillan announced to Parliament the Government's decision to seek to join the EC. In words that resonate just as powerfully today, he said that "our right place is in the vanguard of the move towards the greater unity of the world and we can lead better from within rather than outside."

Sadly for Britain, the President of France, General Charles de Gaulle, was determined to keep his former wartime colleague out of the EC. On 14th January 1963, in an eloquent speech at the Élysée Palace, the general refused on the grounds that the UK was not yet sufficiently 'European'. He may have been right about that, but in my view his main motive was to ensure French leadership of Europe. Four years later, de Gaulle made the same argument in rejecting the attempt of the Labour Prime Minister Harold Wilson to join. By 1970, when, following de Gaulle's resignation a year earlier and Wilson's defeat in the June 1970 general election, the

Heath administration reopened negotiations, the direction of the EC had already been shaped by a historic compromise between France and Germany. In return for accepting protection for French farmers in the form of the Common Agricultural Policy (CAP) as well as French leadership in Europe, the Germans gained a guarantee of access to the industrial markets of the other member states as well as a treaty of friendship with France.

I strongly supported Edward Heath's decision to seek British membership. He rightly took the view that the only way to get the EC to reflect British interests was to change it from within. So, with the support of the new French President, Georges Pompidou (who had succeeded de Gaulle), Heath successfully concluded negotiations with the EC in June 1971. Heath now had to obtain British parliamentary approval. However, there was a determined group of anti-European Tory rebels whose number (about 40) was likely to be greater than the Conservative majority. Heath would need the backing of a number of Labour MPs if he were to get British entry through Parliament.

If Labour had won the 1970 election, it is likely that Wilson would have tried to obtain entry into the EC. But in opposition, it was a different story: Labour opportunistically opposed Heath's proposal. However, a group of pro-European Labour MPs, led by the deputy leader, Roy Jenkins, voted for the principle of entry and defied a Labour three-line whip against the so-called Tory terms. Arguably, this pro-European Labour rebellion was a forerunner to the Social Democratic Party (SDP) breakaway of the early 1980s.

Elected to parliament as a Labour MP at a by-election

in March 1973, I was – to my regret – too late to join the 69 Labour rebels, but I applauded their courage and was delighted by the impressive 112 Commons majority for entry. To me, Heath was justified in claiming in his memoirs that the parliamentary vote for British membership of the EC was his greatest success as prime minister.

The question of whether the UK should stay in the EC – enshrined in Labour's February 1974 election manifesto, which promised either an election or a referendum – was the outstanding issue of Wilson's two governments of the 1970s. If Wilson was to win the referendum to keep the UK in the EC, it was essential to achieve what he could plausibly claim was a successful renegotiation. The visit of Helmut Schmidt, the German Chancellor, to the UK in November 1974 proved decisive.

As a Labour MP, I heard Schmidt's address to the Labour Party conference. Speaking in fluent English, he asked delegates to remember that Labour's sister parties on the continent wanted the UK to remain in the EC, as indeed they still do today. Schmidt followed his moving speech, which received a standing ovation, with talks with Wilson at Chequers, convincing the Prime Minister that there could be a positive outcome to the negotiations, as well as helping to arrange a bilateral meeting between Wilson and the new French President, Valéry Giscard d'Estaing.

In March 1975, following the Dublin European Council summit, Wilson and the Foreign Secretary at the time, James Callaghan, were able to announce that the negotiations had been a success, highlighting small but concrete achievements such as the improved deal for New Zealand and the way in which the controversial UK contribution to the EC budget would now be related to gross national product. In contrast to David Cameron in 2016, Wilson skilfully outlined a pragmatic case for continuing British membership. Mixing his metaphors, he argued that the UK could not retain its world influence "by taking our bat home and sinking into an offshore mentality." The avuncular, low-key approach by Labour's popular leader undoubtedly swayed his party's voters, who might otherwise have been uncertain. What a contrast to Jeremy Corbyn's failure to lead Labour effectively during the 2016 referendum!

Campaigning for Britain in Europe (the official body for pro-Europeans at the time), I became increasingly confident that we would win the 1975 referendum. In the late 1960s and 1970s, the opinion polls – influenced first by de Gaulle's veto and then by the unpopularity of the Heath government – had shown a consistent if shallow-based majority against membership. However, when the referendum forced voters to answer the question 'Do you think that the United Kingdom should stay in the European Community?', opinion shifted and the final result was two to one for staying in.

The pro-European campaign was, in fact, in a much stronger position than the campaign against Europe, not only financially but – more importantly – because most of the respected figures in public life were on their side. Jenkins was president of Britain in Europe, with Willie Whitelaw, Reginald Maudling and Heath serving as vice presidents for the Tories and Jeremy Thorpe and Jo Grimond doing the same for the Liberals. The Confederation of British Industry (CBI), the Trades Union Congress (TUC) and virtually all of the press (except the *Morning Star*) argued for a 'yes' win. On the opposite side, less trusted dissidents such as Tony Benn, Michael Foot and Enoch Powell may have been eloquent, but their warnings about the dangers of the EC did not carry conviction with voters.

There were other underlying issues. The uncertain economic and political background was definitely significant. Christopher Soames, former Tory minister and ambassador to Paris and at the time a British Commissioner, was quoted as saying: "This is not the time for Britain to be considering leaving a Christmas Club, let alone the Common Market." According to Gallup, another issue that was important in persuading people that they were better in than out was the need to strengthen Britain's position in the world. Significantly, many of my north-east constituents said to me that, though they themselves were personally ambivalent, they would vote 'yes' for the sake of their children and grandchildren.

As we sat in our garden listening to the results, I felt that perhaps the British had at long last realised that it was more sensible for a medium-sized European power to join its continental neighbours than to continue to stand alone. The future seemed bright, especially for my generation.

Reluctant Europeans

In parliament, Europe became one of my main preoccupations. I worked hard to bring the Labour Party (which, under Foot, had fought the 1983 election as an anti-European party) to a pro-European position. I also tried to strengthen Labour's links with its sister parties in Europe, regularly attending meetings and conferences across the continent. In the UK, I made frequent speeches and wrote articles and books on European issues, such was my passion to shore up support for British membership and to secure the UK's place at the heart of Europe.

However, despite the results of the 1975 referendum, the British remained reluctant Europeans, sceptical about the benefits of the union. According to the Eurobarometer poll, for most of the years of the UK's membership, only a minority actually thought that it was a 'good thing', a lower percentage than for any other member state.

In 1992, I wrote a book titled *Offshore: Britain and the European Idea* in which I discussed the issues that have shaped negative popular attitudes to continental Europe, including our historical experience and the persisting image of ourselves as an offshore island, separate from the continent. I had hoped that other factors such as trade, travel, employment and education would gradually change opinion – and to some extent they have, particularly amongst the younger generations. But, as demonstrated by the 2016 referendum result, the forces working against wholehearted commitment remained strong, especially in the older generations.

Pro-Europeans point to the malign role of the media – especially *The Sun*, *The Daily Telegraph* and *The Daily Mail*, which at the time of the 1975 referendum had been pro-Europe – in helping create an atmosphere hostile to the EU. There is no doubt that changes in ownership and editorship, as well as their highly cynical exploitation of populist sentiment, were significant. But, in my view, the main culprits were the politicians, above all the party leaders. Instead of making the case for Europe, they tended to run scared, especially of the Murdoch press. Playing to the gallery, they portrayed EU negotiations as a bloody battle with the 'Eurocrats' of Brussels or with 'anti-British' foreign politicians rather than as a constructive exercise in helping achieve what was best for the EU and Europe as a whole.

If things went well in Europe, it was a victory for Britain and British Prime Ministers. If there were problems, it was the fault of Brussels. Our leaders almost never spent time explaining the benefits of British membership or arguing for the EU.

The failure of the politicians
Although the Wilson government had presided over the successful 1975 referendum, Europe remained a divisive issue for the Labour Party. Within five years of the referendum, the party – led by the Bennite left, which had always argued that the EC was an anti-democratic capitalist conspiracy – adopted a policy of outright rejection. Withdrawal became one of the key issues in Labour's 'civil wars' and a major cause

of the SDP breakaway led by Roy Jenkins, Shirley Williams, David Owen and Bill Rodgers, which seriously weakened the Labour Party in the early 1980s. Indeed, Labour fought the June 1983 election – in which it was decisively defeated – on a pledge to take Britain out of the EC "within the lifetime of a Labour government".

I ignored Labour's manifesto pledge, as well as the blandishments of the SDP, and with my wife I wrote a book on European socialist parties, *Socialists in the Recession* (1986), which sought to show that these parties had been more electorally successful than the insular British Labour Party despite the recession of the 1980s. With the support of Denis Healey, then Labour's Shadow Foreign Secretary, we were able to meet some of the European socialist leaders, including my two heroes: the German SPD giants Willy Brandt and Helmut Schmidt. At our dinner table, the charismatic Spanish socialist leader Felipe González described how he was taken out of the Cortes chamber by an attempted coup of right-wing army officers. He thought he was going to be shot. He and his advisers saw Spanish entry into the EC as a democratic bulwark against the enduring threat of military takeover. Subsequently, the EC played a key role in the move towards democracy in Spain, Portugal and Greece.

From the opposition benches, I watched Margaret Thatcher with fascination and some misgivings, especially when she reported on European summits. At the time of the 1975 referendum, she had supported British entry into the EC, and at that time even wore a pullover covered in European flags. There were undoubted successes to her credit, including reducing the cost of the UK's membership ("getting our money back"), the creation of the single market (a Conservative achievement that today's Eurosceptics have conveniently forgotten) and keeping our contributions for agricultural support in check. In her 1988 Bruges speech, she said that "our destiny" was in Europe as part of the EC, though she also warned that "we have not successfully rolled back the frontiers of the state in Britain only to see them reinforced at a European level with a European super-state exercising a new dominance from Brussels."

But one of Thatcher's main problems over the EC was her inimitable style. Too often, she sounded like a warrior queen who had gone out to do battle with Brussels and had come back victorious over her enemies. I shall never forget her statement to the Commons on 30th October 1990 when she made a passionate attack on economic and monetary union, claiming that it was a threat to national identity and parliamentary sovereignty, and concluded with the words "No. No. No." Two days later, her cabinet colleague Lord Howe (then Sir Geoffrey Howe) resigned. In an electrifying speech (perhaps the most dramatic of my time in parliament), he said that he was deeply anxious that "the mood you have struck will make it more difficult for Britain to hold and retain a position of influence in this vital debate." Indeed, Howe's resignation speech set in motion the train of events leading to Thatcher's downfall.

Meanwhile, the Labour Party, under its leader Neil Kinnock (later to become an EU commissioner), began to shift towards a pro-European position. He said that continuing talk of withdrawal was, in his view, "self-defeating". Acting with admirable determination, he built up contacts with European statesmen and party leaders such as Brandt, González and Rocard, while the eloquent speech by the President of the European Commission, Jacques Delors, to the 1988 TUC conference helped win over the British labour movement. In May 1989, the Labour Party's policy review committed it to a new pro-European position: "We want the British people to get the best from the European Community."

A turning point was the 1989 European elections. While the Conservative Party fought a highly negative campaign, directing its fire as much against Brussels as against the Labour Party, Labour argued that a more constructive European approach would bring tangible social benefits to the British people. The results were a kick in the teeth for the Tories and a significant boost for Labour, which increased its representation in the European Parliament to 45 seats, thus forming the biggest bloc in the socialist group. Thatcher had played the anti-European card and been defeated. To my delight, it seemed as if the British now wanted their government to take a more positive line on Europe, though admittedly Thatcher's growing unpopularity was also a factor.

Succeeding Thatcher as Prime Minister, John Major made his first speech on Europe to the Konrad Adenauer Foundation in Bonn, in which he said: "My aims for Britain in the Community could be simply stated. I want us to be where we belong. At the very heart of Europe, working with our partners in building the future." But though the Major government abandoned Thatcher's isolationism, it was slow in coming forward with constructive ideas of its own. One commentator even wrote: "The Prime Minister continues to give the impression of backing into Europe somewhat in the manner of a gate-crasher entering a party by pretending he is going home." The problem for Major was that his hesitant Europeanism was too much for some of his vocal Conservative Eurosceptic critics, but too little to help secure British interests in the EC.

In a sporting cliché, he (or at least his spokesman) proclaimed that the result of the European Council meeting at Maastricht in December 1991, in which he obtained two opt-out clauses, was "game, set and match for Britain". In fact, the main purpose of the two opt-outs (one from the single currency, the other from the European Social Chapter) was to obtain an agreement that he could sell to Conservative anti-Europeans. But, in giving priority to pacifying his party, he left the UK isolated in Europe. The eventual passage of the Maastricht treaty through Parliament only came after months of fierce Conservative infighting. This was the beginning of an enduring Eurosceptic rebellion inside the Tory Party, which effectively prevented the Major government from playing a constructive European role and eventually – I will argue – led to Brexit.

At about this time, my own role and activity on the European issue increased considerably. I spoke frequently inside the Commons chamber and at parliamentary Labour Party meetings, and was in demand on television and radio. At the European Movement's AGM in March 1995, I was elected as chairman and attacked the Eurosceptics for their "failure to concern themselves with the national interest", a criticism still applicable to today's Brexiteers.

During the Maastricht debates, I was sent to the continent by the Labour Party. Speaking in Copenhagen during the second Danish referendum (which was won by the pro-European campaign, though only after unexpectedly losing the first), I put forward the positive case for the Maastricht Treaty. I denounced Norman Tebbit and William Cash, who were assisting the Danish anti-Europeans, as being "xenophobic meddlers, fighting British battles on Danish soil", and even managed to make a reference to Hamlet: "Like Rosencrantz and Guildenstern, they are not as they seem. They are using the Danes for their own purposes." A few months earlier, I had spoken at a meeting during the French referendum at Céret in the foothills of the Pyrenees. Coached in French by my two young nephews (who lived in the south-west), I assured the audience of the importance of a French 'yes' vote: "*Tous les regards d'Europe sont orientés vers la France. Nous comptons sur vous.*" Fortunately, François Mitterrand (with the support of Paris) narrowly won the referendum.

1989 was the miraculous year when the Soviet Empire collapsed and a democratic revolution swept across eastern Europe. In Poland, my wife's birthplace, lengthy negotiations between the Polish trade union Solidarity and the communist regime led to democratic elections for the senate and for a proportion of the lower house. Solidarity swept the board, and Tadeusz Mazowiecki became the first non-communist Prime Minister in eastern Europe since the fall of the Iron Curtain. In Hungary, the Communist Party accepted a multi-party system and opened its borders, while on 9th November, the charismatic Soviet leader Mikhail Gorbachev visited East Germany and told the local communists that they could no longer rely on Soviet support. Then, after widespread demonstrations in the main East German cities, the unthinkable happened:

the Berlin Wall came down. In December, the Velvet Revolution swept the communists from power in Czechoslovakia, while at the end of the year, the Romanians overthrew Nicolae Ceaușescu.

I was an enthralled observer of these great events taking place in Central and Eastern Europe. With my friend George Robertson, later Secretary General of NATO, I walked through the Brandenburg Gate into East Berlin, buying a piece of the Wall on the way back. After all these years as a symbol of division, Berlin was now 'open'. My wife and I were also in Prague when that beautiful city was in the midst of its first free elections. Everywhere, there were posters of Tomáš Masaryk, the first President of independent Czechoslovakia, alongside the country's new President, Václav Havel.

Over the following few years, I met newly elected MPs from Poland, Hungary and the Baltic states, all of whom were enthusiastic both for democracy and for their countries to join the EC. The British Association for Central and Eastern Europe (BACEE), of which I became the chairman, was expertly directed by two ex-ambassadors, Sir John Birch and Nicholas Jarrold. It held training courses, seminars and conferences, mostly devoted to preparing these countries for accession to the EU. It was an exciting and constructive time.

I also rejoiced when the Labour Party won the 1997 UK election in a landslide victory. Quite apart from ending 18 years in opposition, Tony Blair was the most pro-European British Prime Minister, at least since Heath. Blair had voted 'yes' in the 1975 referendum, he took his holidays in France and Italy and his command of French was good enough to speak directly to MPs in the French National Assembly. Before the election, he told me that his ambition was to reconcile the British to membership of the EU and for the UK to play a cooperative part in its workings. At Aachen in the summer of 1999, Blair spoke publicly of this aim, saying he hoped that "over the next few years Britain resolves once and for all its ambivalence towards Europe. I want to end the uncertainty, the lack of confidence, the Europhobia."

The new Prime Minister had made a good start. At his first Intergovernmental Conference at Amsterdam, the youthful Blair established warm relations with the leaders of the other member states. Lord John Kerr, then the Foreign Office Permanent Secretary, commented that Blair had enjoyed Amsterdam and found that he had a "real flair" for European negotiations.

The British government supported enlargement, a process that was brought to a formal conclusion in 2004 when the EU had reached 25 member states. (However, seriously underestimating the level of immigration from eastern Europe, Britain – unlike France and Germany – did not seek a transition period. This would ultimately be to the cost of the future Remain campaign). The UK also helped initiate the Lisbon agenda of economic reform to make the EU more flexible and innovative. In December 1998, together with French President Jacques Chirac, Blair launched a joint Anglo-French initiative on European defence. These were the actions of a Prime Minister determined to end Britain's isolation and play a leading role in the EU.

By this time, I was chairman of the House of Commons Treasury Committee and was able to use this influential position, as well as my chairmanship of the European Movement, to try to help create a national, cross-party, pro-European campaign. My access to No. 10 and No. 11 Downing Street and my good relations with pro-European Tories such as Ken Clarke, and Liberal Democrats including Menzies Campbell and Charles Kennedy, were useful assets in this aim. On 14th October 1999, the Britain in Europe campaign was launched, with Blair joined by the Tory 'big beasts' Ken Clarke and Michael Heseltine, as well as by Gordon Brown and Robin Cook from the Labour Party and the Liberal Democrat leader at the time, Charles Kennedy. This was the high point of cross-party cooperation on Europe. From the first, however, there was an ambivalence about the Labour government's position, which was to make campaigning for the euro or the case for the UK's membership of the EU extremely difficult.

The decision not to join the single currency in the first wave inevitably hampered the Blair administration's efforts to act as a leader in Europe. Despite Blair's constructive EU initiatives and his warm words about the euro, he was not prepared to take any risks over Europe in case they aroused the hostility of the Murdoch press, thereby jeopardising his prospects of winning a second term, which was his main concern. Blair also wanted to avoid a head-on clash with his chancellor, Brown, who despite being more enthusiastic about the euro than Blair in opposition, changed his mind in government, partly in case his support of the euro would reduce his chances of succeeding Blair as Prime Minister. In my Foreign Policy Centre pamphlet *How to Join the Euro*, I accepted the need for what the Treasury termed sustainable convergence between the UK and the euro area, but argued that there was still a strong case for joining both on economic and political grounds and that, outside the euro, the UK's ability to influence the future shape of the EU would remain seriously limited.

It was a source of great sadness for me that, despite being a pro-European and the finest communicator of his generation, Blair seemed so reluctant to make the case for Europe directly to the British people. Neither Blair nor Brown made any contribution to Labour's abysmal campaign in the 1999 European elections, in which, on a low turnout, Labour won only 29 seats to the Tories' 36. And when, at a meeting in No. 10, I showed Blair Labour's national election material with the extraordinary slogan 'What did you ever get out of Europe?', he could only shake his head (though he had earlier agreed to join the Britain in Europe campaign).

Blair's best speeches on Europe were made outside this country, in Warsaw and in Strasbourg, in which he warned the European Parliament, "The people are blowing trumpets around the city walls." In the UK, though, he failed to stand up to the growing tide of Euroscepticism. In a private meeting, I warned him that, if he took part in the invasion of Iraq, it could not only weaken his position in Europe, but it could also make it more difficult to win over the British people for the European cause. Sure enough, after Iraq, Blair's influence sadly waned, so much so that, by the time of the 2016 referendum, his sensible advice was often ignored.

As Prime Minister, Brown was even more cautious than Blair. He used the Treasury's negative assessment of joining the euro in 2003 to kick the issue into the long grass. He was also criticised for his clumsy handling of the signing of the Lisbon Treaty in 2007 – he flew to Lisbon only to deliberately miss the signing ceremony – as well as for the negotiations in

November 2009 over the President of the Council and the EU High Representative. That said, the French President Nicolas Sarkozy and the German Chancellor Angela Merkel respected Brown both for his leadership during the world financial crisis and his reliability as a British ally.

If the cautious Europeanism of Blair and Brown had disappointed their supporters, the pragmatic Euroscepticism of the Conservative leader David Cameron failed to satisfy either the growing body of ideological Eurosceptics or the dwindling band of pro-Europeans in the Tory Party. For Cameron, this would eventually lead to both personal and national disaster.

To win the Tory leadership in 2005, Cameron had cynically been prepared to pull the Conservative Party out of the centre-right European People's Party grouping on the grounds that it was too 'federalist' – a move which, by infuriating his main continental ally, Angela Merkel, was to cost him dearly. But in his first conference speech in 2006, Cameron warned his party to "stop banging on about Europe". The 2010 general election saw the Conservatives form a coalition with the Liberal Democrats, which gave Cameron some protection against the growing demands of Tory Eurosceptic backbenchers. And though the commitments to Europe contained in the joint coalition programme stated that no further powers would be transferred to Brussels without a referendum, it also said that Britain would "play a leading role in an enlarged European Union".

At first, this compromise between Cameron and Liberal Democrat leader Nick Clegg enabled Britain to operate as a relatively effective member of the EU. However, in October 2011, 81 Tory MPs defied a three-line whip by supporting a motion in favour of an 'in-out' referendum on European membership, an act of rebellion which clearly rattled an already nervous Prime Minister. Just over a year later, in January 2013, Cameron made a keynote speech in the London Bloomberg office which he hoped would put to bed the Tory Party's internal row over Europe until after the upcoming general election. In this speech, he promised both "fundamental EU reform" and a disastrous, as it turned out, in-out referendum on the UK's membership.

From the opposition backbenches in the Lords, I watched the Tory Prime Minister's response to his backbench critics with growing apprehension. When faced with Eurosceptic demands, Cameron nearly always seemed to concede, though this never satisfied his critics, most of whom were now determined that, at whatever the cost to the country, Britain should leave the EU.

Though Cameron presided over the successful campaign for Scotland to remain part of the UK in 2014 (in which Brown and the former Labour Chancellor Alistair Darling had, in fact, played the leading roles), I had no confidence in his ability to persuade the continental Europeans to give the British a 'special' deal, nor to lead the Remain voters to victory. Until the 2015 election, Cameron had been protected by his Liberal Democrat coalition partners, but once the Tories won the 2015 election outright – virtually wiping out the Liberal Democrats – his rash pledge to hold a referendum quickly plunged Britain into dangerous waters.

In 2016, the Leavers were much stronger than in 1975. In contrast to the 1975 referendum campaign, there was now an 82 per cent press circulation advantage in favour of Brexit. The

Leave campaign was also greatly strengthened not only by the support of many Tory MPs, but crucially by the last-minute and opportunist adherence of two Conservative heavy-weights: Boris Johnson and Michael Gove. Fear of immigration also played into the hands of the Leavers, a fear that was unscrupulously exploited by the Leave campaign which went so far as to claim – totally mendaciously – that Turkey was about to join the EU.

Overconfident and increasingly unpopular (especially with Labour voters), Cameron fought a poor campaign. Having already promised the Tory Party that he would "sort out" immigration, he had failed to persuade European leaders, above all the German Chancellor, to make any substantial concessions. Perhaps, if he had insisted on some kind of 'emergency brake' during his discussions with the Europeans, he might have been able to blunt the immigration issue, especially if it had been backed up by a special immigration fund to help affected areas. But ignoring the issue, as Cameron eventually decided to do, ultimately played into the hands of the Leavers. It was not enough for the Remainers to repeat warnings from the Treasury, the Bank of England and international business about the economic risks posed by Brexit. In the end, the Leave campaign was able to dismiss these concerns as 'Project Fear'. When the chancellor George Osborne published his plans for an emergency post-referendum budget, which contained tax increases of £15 billion, it was simply not believed. And although Cameron and Osborne were advised that concentrating solely on the economic costs without making a positive case for Europe was turning off younger voters, who needed to be persuaded to come out and vote, the two leaders failed to react. There was almost no mention of the EU's support for peace in Europe and its backing for democracy in southern Europe and the Balkans, let alone the economic, social, environmental and security advantages that membership had brought to the UK.

Cameron got little help from the Labour leader, Corbyn, whose contribution to the campaign was, at best, half-hearted. Former Labour cabinet minister and EU Trade Commissioner Peter Mandelson put it this way: "We were greatly damaged by Jeremy Corbyn's stance; not only was he most of the time absent from the fight, but he was holding back the efforts of Alan Johnson and the Labour campaign." Despite their leader's lacklustre performance, two thirds of Labour voters supported Remain on 23rd June, which was, after all, party policy. If Corbyn – for much of his political career a left-wing Eurosceptic – had put more effort into the campaign, the referendum could have been won.

All in all, the result of the 2016 referendum represented a massive failure by the country's political leadership. As the political commentator Andrew Marr concluded, "It was the biggest establishment cock-up of my lifetime." I wholeheartedly agreed with him. We were reaping what we had sown.

Brexit

The day after the 2016 referendum, the depression my wife and I felt at the result was greatly increased by the reaction of our children and grandchildren, whose mood was a combination of anger and despair. But their harsh judgment was not quite fair. I knew that my family had voted to remain, but I was also aware that, though young people under 24 had voted overwhelmingly against Brexit, their turnout compared unfavourably with that of the over-60s. My grandchildren later confirmed that a number of their friends had not 'bothered' to vote, either because of exams or holiday plans or because they thought the result was a foregone conclusion. The result, then, was shaped both by the heavier voting of the over-60s and by the failure of too many young voters to vote at all.

That same day, we were also surprised by the appearance of the two chief Leavers, Boris Johnson and Michael Gove, on television. Their reaction was seemingly one of shock and confusion. They had clearly not expected the Leave campaign to win, nor Cameron to resign. It was also clear that they had little idea of what leaving the EU entailed. Johnson – who, after all, had been the big figure of the Leave campaign – had the chutzpah, a few days later (in an article in *The Telegraph*), to call upon the government to come forward with a post-Brexit plan. The cheek of the man! His subsequent record, and that of many other Brexiteers, has shown that Leavers had no convincing alternative to British membership of the EU. No wonder, then, that Donald Tusk, the able pro-British President of the European Council, would later say that there was a "special place in Hell" for people who "promoted Brexit without a plan".

In the first House of Lords debate on the outcome of the referendum, I accepted the validity of the result, though with reluctance and sadness. I also stated that both Leavers and Remainers had a duty "to work our way through the linked crises that face us and try to produce long-term policies in the national interest". I argued that it was right to delay invoking Article 50 (which set out the process for withdrawal) until we had a proper plan and stressed the importance of retaining access to the EU "which is by far our biggest market". I also rejected the idea – put forward by the previous speaker, the former Tory Chancellor Lord Lawson – of leaving the single market. After referring to the crisis in the Tory Party and the lack of confidence many Labour MPs had in their leader, I underlined the importance of the role of parliament in overseeing Brexit plans, the invoking of Article 50 and subsequent negotiations. I concluded by saying, "In times of national crisis, when government and parties have been found wanting, we have to turn to our national parliament for advice and help."

On 13th July – after a bizarre Tory leadership election in which one leading candidate, Gove, stabbed his former ally, Johnson, in the back – the Home Secretary, Theresa May, emerged as Prime Minister. She saw her main task as being to take the UK out of the EU. The unanswered question, however, was how she was going to do it.

The UK had voted to leave the EU, but had indicated

neither how this was to be done, nor what our relationship with the EU was to look like; in the words of Mandelson, "The future relationship was not on the ballot paper." May had been a Remainer, albeit a reluctant one. Would she come down on the side of the Eurosceptics and go for a 'hard' Brexit? Or would she be a pragmatic national leader, above warring factions, reaching out beyond party boundaries to pursue the best possible deal for her country?

The UK's prosperity inside the EU has been partly based on the volume (over 40 per cent) of exports to other member states, as well as its 40 per cent share of EU inward investment. Foreign companies have come to the UK as a base for trading within the EU. Like Germany, the UK has also used its membership of the EU to facilitate its entry into global markets. Indeed, the trade deal brokered between the EU and Japan in February 2019 shows the far-reaching advantages that EU membership can bring. The UK's position within the EU has also been buttressed by special opt-outs, the prime examples being the single currency and the Schengen Agreement. The main purpose of Brexit negotiations should, therefore, have been to protect these great advantages as far as possible by remaining close to the EU.

At the start of her premiership, many were prepared to give May the benefit of the doubt. My old friend Ken Clarke, the Conservative pro-European, might have memorably called her "a bloody difficult woman", but I was impressed by her speech outside No. 10 Downing Street in which she promised to fight against the glaring injustices of "poverty, race, class and health" and to make Britain "a country that works for everybody". It was understandable that, alongside prominent

Remainers such as Philip Hammond, she should appoint three leading Brexiteers to her Cabinet, though not in the positions she gave them. I was sure that the erratic Johnson would be a flop as Foreign Secretary and that Liam Fox, an anti-European ideologue, would be a poor choice as International Trade Secretary. From my time in the Commons, I knew the Secretary of State for Exiting the EU, David Davis, as an easy-going performer; he had been Major's Europe Minister, but he also had a reputation for resigning when the going got tough, as it was bound to do during the negotiations.

And as the months went by, I began to have serious misgivings about the Prime Minister herself. May was slow to reveal her negotiating strategy. Just repeating that "Brexit means Brexit" – a remark she first made during her campaign for the Tory leadership – may have been fine as a soundbite to appease the Brexiteers in her party, but it did not even begin to add up to a convincing approach to negotiation.

Then, in her party conference speeches, May announced that she would convert the existing body of European law into British law, through a bill that would eventually become the European Union (Withdrawal) Bill. She pledged to trigger Article 50 by the end of March 2017 – an unwise move that gave her government only two years for their negotiations. As the EU negotiator Michel Barnier said, "The clock is ticking." May also made it clear that the authority of European law in Britain would end. In other words, the jurisdiction of the European Court of Justice would cease. This may have pleased Eurosceptics, but it appalled British pro-Europeans. It was a clear sign that, in order to appease the Brexiteers, the Prime Minister would come down on the side of a 'hard' Brexit.

On 17th January 2017, May made a keynote speech at Lancaster House. It had been her usual practice to announce policy through the medium of set-piece addresses, and the Lancaster House speech was billed as setting out the government's objectives for exiting the EU. In that respect, it was little short of a disaster.

The Prime Minister began by making friendly gestures towards the EU, saying that "our vote to leave the European Union was no rejection of the values we share". She added that "we will continue to be reliable partners, willing allies and close friends", a commitment which – in view of Brexit – her partners might have had reason to doubt. She even went as far as to assure other EU member states that "we are leaving the European Union, but we are not leaving Europe". As if we could. However, the main purpose of May's speech was to please the Brexiteers in her party. She reaffirmed that her government would end the jurisdiction of the European Court of Justice in Britain. She also made it clear that the UK would leave the single market. (It is a strange irony that, in 1988, another Tory Prime Minister – Thatcher – had announced in that same building her intention to take Britain *into* the single market, a hugely successful policy that was partly her idea.) In addition, May said that she did not want Britain to remain a member of the customs union. These commitments were her 'red lines' – that is, lines that were not to be crossed. They could have been lifted straight from a Eurosceptic pamphlet; as such, they would make it impossible to achieve a deal that would be in the national interest.

Certainly, the Prime Minister proclaimed lofty generalisations such as "we will pursue a bold and ambitious free trade agreement with the European Union" and "we must reach a completely new customs union". She also stated: "I want us to be a truly global Britain." Fine sentiments, but there was little indication of how these ambitions were to be achieved. May also made the claim that "no deal for Britain is better than a bad deal for Britain". The House of Lords EU committee dealt with that foolish assertion by pointing out that 'no deal' would be a disaster for the whole country, a verdict that has subsequently been supported by businesses, the City, the Bank of England, the Treasury, the overwhelming majority of economists and now the House of Commons.

One possible chink of light was that May recognised that there would have to be a two-year transitional period after the Article 50 procedure had come to an end in order to avoid a 'cliff edge', which would be highly disruptive, especially for business. However, Lord Bridges, a government minister who later resigned, called a transitional period without an agreement on a future relationship with the EU "a gangplank into thin air".

Concluding her keynote speech, the Prime Minister announced that the government would put the final deal to a vote in both Houses of Parliament. But, despite all their fine talk about restoring parliamentary sovereignty, the Brexiteers were extremely worried about involving parliament in the process of leaving: they had no majority in the Commons and were only a minority in the Lords.

Unwisely, the government tried to trigger Article 50 without parliamentary approval. When the High Court ruled that the government did not possess the power to do so, the Eurosceptic press denounced the three High Court judges, with the *Daily Mail* outrageously calling them "Enemies of the People". The Supreme Court subsequently confirmed the High Court ruling, forcing the government to introduce a two-clause bill to legalise the triggering of Article 50. It passed through both Houses of Parliament, and on 29th March 2017, the Prime Minister signed the letter that set the Article 50 process in motion – a sad day for Remainers that even brought tears to the eyes of Tusk.

Then, although May had pledged not to have an early general election, she was persuaded by her chief ministers and advisers to call a 'snap' election, to be held on 8th June that year. Her argument was that she needed to strengthen her position both in parliament and at the Brexit negotiation table.

The decision turned out to be a disaster for her. May proved to be a poor campaigner. By contrast, Corbyn – who the previous year had comfortably survived the attempt by rebellious moderate Labour MPs to unseat him – was in his element. While May appeared wooden and robotic, Corbyn came across as warm and energetic, offering a message of hope to large and enthusiastic meetings of grassroots supporters. And the results showed it. Instead of gaining the 60 seats they had expected, the Tories lost 13 and – more importantly – their overall majority. Labour, despite experiencing another defeat, gained 30 seats, increasing their share of the total vote to 40 per cent.

After the election, May managed to cobble together a minority government with the Northern Irish Democratic Unionist Party (DUP), but her position still looked rocky, especially after her seemingly unfeeling response to the Grenfell Tower disaster. Without a clear majority, she ought to have changed strategy and tried to appeal to Labour and the other opposition parties in order to establish a cross-party consensus. However, despite a lacklustre speech at the Conservative party conference, May survived as Prime Minister – mainly because there was no agreement on a successor.

Meanwhile, the 'divorce' talks between Davis and Barnier, which continued throughout the summer, had got nowhere. May's next big speech, made in September 2017 in the church of Santa Maria Novella in Florence, was an attempt to break the deadlock by setting a more constructive tone. She repeated her mantra: "We may be leaving the European Union, but we are not leaving Europe." With regard to the negotiations, May made it clear that the British government would not "accept any physical infrastructure at the border" between the Republic of Ireland and the North (though she gave no indication as to how this was to be achieved). She also stressed the need to protect the rights of European nationals living in the UK and British nationals living in the 27 member states of the EU, and she wisely promised that the UK would honour financial commitments made during the period of British membership.

The British government's concessions, set out in the Florence speech, led to agreement in principle on the first phase of Brexit. There was also an acceptance on both sides of the need for a transition period (which May confusingly called an implementation period) during which the UK, in most aspects, would remain an EU member. She described it as a double lock, "a guarantee that there will be a period of implementation giving businesses and people certainty that they will be able to prepare for the change; and a guarantee that this period will be time limited".

But the glaring weakness of the Florence speech – and, later, the Mansion House address, which she gave the following March – was her failure to answer the key question of the UK's future economic relationship with the EU. The difficulty for the Prime Minister was that, in her Lancaster House speech, she had already ruled out the possibility of the UK remaining a member of either the single market or the customs union. As a result, the UK would not be able to adopt the 'Norway model' of remaining in the single market, despite May's admission that leaving the single market would significantly reduce UK access to EU markets. However, the 'Canada model' for a free trade agreement, also mooted, would provide only limited provision for services – so important for the British economy – and would also fail to provide an open border between Ireland and Northern Ireland. Instead, May talked of a "bespoke" agreement for the UK, an arrangement that has not – so far – been accepted by the EU. Fox's former permanent secretary, Sir Martin Donnelly, remarked that leaving the single market and the customs union was like "giving up a three-course meal now for the promise of a packet of crisps in the future". The reality, of course, is that there is no trading deal with Europe that would be an improvement on the one Britain already enjoys as a member of the EU.

With the government confused and divided over Brexit, the Labour opposition was ambivalent. The majority of Labour voters were Remainers, but Corbyn was still a Eurosceptic, and he also faced pressure from Leave-voting Labour constituencies. However, the shadow Brexit Secretary, Sir Keir Starmer, skilfully nudged the party into a stronger, more realistic position. At the party conference in September 2017, a wide-ranging motion was carried which added backing for full participation in the single market. And at the 2018 party conference, it was Starmer again who insisted on leaving open the option of a 'confirmatory' referendum.

Meanwhile in the Lords, in April and May 2018, Labour – ably led by Angela Smith and Dianne Hayter and working with other opposition parties, cross-benchers and Tory dissidents – inflicted a series of defeats on the government through 14 successful amendments to the Withdrawal Bill. These included overwhelming support for a customs union, preserving the 'open' border between Northern Ireland and the Republic (as established by the Good Friday Agreement) and giving parliament a meaningful say on Brexit. Against the advice of the two frontbenches in the Lords, peers also narrowly voted for staying in the European Economic Area (on the lines of the Norway model), though an attempt to write in a second referendum was defeated. On this last point, I abstained – not because I was against a second referendum in principle, but because I thought it was too soon. I felt that a second vote so quickly after the first might not be conclusive. However, as time went on, the lack of a parliamentary majority for other proposals made a second referendum more attractive.

The significance of what was happening in the Lords was that it gave new heart to the pro-Europeans and also caused some Brexiteers to reconsider the terms or even the fact of Brexit itself. When the Withdrawal Bill returned to the Commons, the lower house accepted that the government should seek a customs 'arrangement'. In addition, after lengthy and complex negotiations with Tory pro-Remain rebels, it was also agreed that parliament should have a say on any final deal reached with the EU.

May twisted and turned as she vainly attempted to reach a settlement that would be acceptable not only to the Brexiteers, but to the nation as a whole. As negotiations with the EU stalemated and the months until 29th March 2019 kept ticking by, she came forward with a new initiative in the form of a White Paper. The government's White Paper on the future relationship between the UK and the EU was agreed at Chequers by the Cabinet (though it led to the resignations of two leading Brexiteers: Davis and Johnson), and was presented to parliament by the Prime Minister in July 2018.

The White Paper was long overdue – in fact, it should have been produced before May triggered Article 50 – but it was at least an attempt to row back from the 'hard' Brexit approach set out in her January 2017 Lancaster House speech. She claimed that the White Paper "would preserve the UK's and EU's frictionless access to each other's markets for goods, protecting jobs and livelihoods on both sides, and propose new arrangements for services" as well as avoiding a hard border between Northern Ireland and Ireland.

However, the government's position remained unclear on a number of key issues, including a customs union and how to preserve an open border in Ireland. It also aroused strong opposition from hard-line Brexiteers, while the Labour Party argued that the White Paper was too vague and did not go far enough. Above all, it was not acceptable to the EU, as became clear at the Salzburg summit on 20th September 2018.

In November that year, the British government at last

reached a draft agreement with the EU, covering the rights of EU and British citizens; the financial obligations of the UK; keeping the Irish border open (including an insurance 'backstop'); and a transitional period between 29th March 2019 and 30th September 2020 to give business time to adjust. This 'divorce agreement' was accompanied by a much shorter and far less precise non-binding political declaration setting out the framework for the future relationship between the UK and the EU.

May now had to get a majority in the Commons for her deal. But after some delay, on 15th January 2019, MPs overwhelmingly rejected the deal: 432 votes to 202. The DUP and hard-line Brexiteers opposed the Irish border backstop on the grounds that the UK would not be able to end it without the EU's agreement, while Labour and other opposition parties rejected the political declaration as being no more than the 'agenda points' for future negotiations.

When MPs voted again on 29th January, only two amendments were carried: the Brady amendment, calling for the backstop to be replaced by 'alternative arrangements' and for May to return to Brussels to try to secure changes to her original deal; and the cross-party Spellman/Dromey amendment, which rejected the UK leaving the EU without a deal.

A confused and frustrating period followed as May tried to get her deal 'over the line'. In the Lords, a cross-bench peer, Lord Hope, likened it to an aircraft slowly circling round an airport in a holding pattern, vainly seeking a place and a time to land. After fruitless trips to Brussels, the Prime Minister obstinately presented her deal to the Commons once again. But on 12th March, MPs rejected her deal for the second time, this time by 149 votes. In a defiant statement, the Prime Minister unwisely heaped all the blame on MPs.

In response, MPs seized hold of the parliamentary agenda on 25th March by winning a crucial vote to permit a series of so-called 'indicative' ballots. However, none of the eight proposals received an overall majority: Clarke's plan for the UK to join a customs union came closest to a majority, being defeated by only eight votes; the motion for a second 'confirmatory referendum' (brilliantly introduced by Margaret Beckett) received 268 votes but was defeated by 27. Significantly, both received more support than May's deal, while a motion for 'no deal' was decisively defeated.

Then, on 29th March – the day on which the UK was meant to leave the EU – a truncated 'divorce-only' version was defeated by 58 votes, some of the shrewder hard-liners now supporting May as they at last realised the growing danger that Brexit might not be achieved at all. In an act of desperation, the Prime Minister promised to resign if Tory MPs backed her. Before the third vote on her deal, she had also asked EU leaders for a short delay: they agreed on a new date of 12th April. Meanwhile, on 1st April there was a further parliamentary stalemate when MPs' eight original proposals were reduced to four. This time, Clarke's customs union motion was defeated by a mere three votes.

On 2nd April, following a five-hour 'crisis cabinet', May at last made a decisive switch in strategy – a move she arguably ought to have made when she became Prime Minister and certainly when she lost her overall majority following the 2017 election. She announced that she would open negotiations with the Labour Party to try to agree on a joint Brexit plan.

Wisely, Corbyn agreed immediately. However, although both sides said that the talks were being conducted in a constructive spirit, there remained crucial sticking points, including May's so-called 'red lines' and the support for a confirmatory public vote by a majority of Labour MPs. Many commentators thought it unlikely that two politicians, who had so far shown little sign of statesman-like qualities, would produce a deal that was in the interest of the nation as a whole. So it proved. After six weeks, the talks were abandoned without agreement.

In order to secure the necessary time for these new talks, May – who had previously been so insistent on the UK leaving the EU on 29th March – was humiliatingly forced to ask the European leaders for a further extension. The Prime Minister preferred only a short delay – above all, because she wanted to avoid fighting the EU elections. The European Council, once again acting in an impressive show of unity, reiterated that there could be no reopening of the Withdrawal Agreement, but they granted a six-month extension of Article 50, until 31st October. European Council President Tusk's message to his British friends was: "Please do not waste this time."

This pause provided a moment for reflection on the extraordinary events that followed the referendum result in 2016. As Andrew Rawnsley pointed out in the *Observer* on 31st March 2019, May was dealt a bad hand which she played "spectacularly badly". From the first, she failed to reach out to the whole nation, instead concentrating her energies on trying to please the Brexiteer 'ultras' in her own party. Her position was then drastically weakened when she called the unnecessary election in the spring of 2017, in which she lost her majority; May then had to rely on the narrow-minded and obdurate DUP. What made matters even worse for her was that the hard-line Brexiteers, led by the so-called European Research Group (whose chairman was the vainglorious and perfidious Jacob Rees-Mogg), consistently opposed her strategy in favour of a highly dangerous 'no deal' outcome.

On 22nd May, the Prime Minister, in desperation, put forward a so-called 'ten-point' Brexit plan which included a proposal for a Withdrawal Agreement Bill, with the requirement for a vote on whether or not to hold a second referendum. Andrea Leadsom, the Leader of the House, resigned in response and other members of Mrs May's cabinet were outspoken in their rejection of the plan. On 24th May, having finally lost control of her Cabinet and with tears in her eyes, May resigned outside No. 10 Downing Street. It was the fourth Tory premiership – along with those of Thatcher, Major and Cameron – to be destroyed by the European issue.

For pro-Europeans, there was at last a ray of hope. Defeat at the referendum, the arrogance of the Leavers and May's blinkered approach for the first time created a genuine European movement. In the weeks surrounding the initial 29th March deadline, about 6 million people signed a petition to revoke Article 50, and on 23rd March, in one of the largest public demonstrations in history, more than 1 million people marched against Brexit. It is also highly significant that the young – who are, after all, the generations who will live with the consequences of Brexit – are conspicuous in their support for Europe and a second referendum.

On the face of it, the European parliamentary elections of late May were noteworthy for the triumph of Nigel Farage's single-issue Brexit Party (which finished top with 31.6 per cent of the vote), the failure of the ambivalent Labour Party (which came third, with only 14.1 per cent), and the even-more-disastrous performance of the Conservative Party (with under 10 per cent). But another significant feature, underplayed by most of the press, was the success of those parties that advocated remaining in the EU. The Liberal Democrats, with their rude but succinct slogan of 'bollocks to Brexit', came second (with over 20 per cent), while the Green Party (with 12.1 per cent) and the SNP and Plaid Cymru also did well. Indeed, adding the Labour Remainers, the minority of pro-European Tory votes, and the small Change UK vote, the Remain camp probably received over half the total vote. Whilst these European parliamentary election results confirmed the implications of the local elections, that the pro-Europeans were very much back in business, it is also true that the country remains bitterly divided over Brexit and the outcome of a second referendum would be too close to call.

The weeks from the resignation of May to the announcement of the new Conservative leader were dominated by the Tory leadership election. Rory Stewart, with considerable courage and skill, was the only candidate who made a convincing case for a realistic, moderate Brexit during the campaign. Ten candidates were whittled down to two: Boris Johnson and the Foreign Secretary, Jeremy Hunt. Both argued for a no-deal Brexit if necessary. Johnson also promised he would take the UK out of the EU by 31st October 2019, "do or die".

As the 160,000 Conservative Party members decided between the two candidates, the Brexit stance of both candidates hardened, including the wholesale removal of the Irish backstop from any deal. On 23rd July, the celebrity politician Johnson – half cynical opportunist, half outrageous buffoon – won a resounding two-to-one victory and the next day became Prime Minister, the post he had coveted all his political life.

What will Johnson's Brexit strategy be? His first act was to sack more than half of May's cabinet and packed his own top team with hard-line Brexiteers. Immediately, he will try to reach a new deal with the EU. Such a deal would largely be based on the existing May deal, with a few changes – the so-called 'lipstick on the pig'. But with his insistence on the removal of the backstop he is unlikely to succeed. Despite parliamentary opposition, he is then likely to proceed to a potentially disastrous no-deal – which, in any case, remains the default legal position. This could lead to a vote of no confidence in parliament, and possibly a general election. At that point, a second referendum backed by Labour and the Liberal Democrats seems less likely. Whatever happens, the immediate future remains extremely uncertain, not to say bleak.

Conclusion: The Case for EU Membership

Between the passage of the committee and report stages of the European Union (Withdrawal) Bill through the Lords, I returned to the Low Countries where, 60 years before, my love affair with Europe had blossomed. My wife and I spent a week in Flanders, exploring the two wonderful medieval cities of Bruges and Ghent.

The histories of modern Belgium and Britain are, in fact, closely interlinked. In 1830, at the London Conference, Britain and France recognised the independent neutral country of Belgium, and in 1914, Britain declared war on Germany for ignoring Belgium's neutrality by invading her. A substantial part of the bloody 1914–18 war was fought in West Flanders, as the region's 160 British and Commonwealth war cemeteries so graphically and tragically demonstrate – a reminder, if nothing else, that there was no way Britain could isolate itself from a European war. In May 1940, Germany invaded Belgium once again, and it was not until September 1944 that, following the D-Day landings in June of that year, the Allies were able to liberate the country.

Today, Belgium is a close ally and trading partner of the UK. Both countries are members of NATO and – until Brexit happens (if it does) – of the EU as well. Belgium is our eighth-biggest trading partner. Indeed, as May herself has pointed out, the UK exports twice as much to Belgium as it does to

India, a fact that illustrates the fanciful nature of most of the former International Trade Secretary's policies. Conversations with the inhabitants of Bruges and Ghent during our visit show how much goodwill still remains towards Britain. "Why are you doing this?" they asked with incredulity.

Most continentals understand, as too many of the British still do not, that Europe is and will remain our backyard, one in which we will continue to do the main bulk of our trading. As David Lidington, the former Cabinet Office Minister who was de facto deputy to May, reminded hard-line Brexiteers in her Cabinet: "The facts of geography, history, commercial reality are not going to change."

This is not to deny that the EU needs reforming. In the 21st century, it faces a number of massive challenges. These include ensuring sustained economic growth, developing credible policies to combat climate change, controlling immigration and confronting extremist political forces. Beyond its borders to the east, there is the threat from Putin's Russia, while to the west, Trump's unpredictable foreign and protectionist trade policies threaten the post-war international order. But these are not arguments for Britain leaving the EU or – as some Brexiteers even believe – for the EU breaking up altogether. On the contrary, these challenges can only be faced effectively if Europeans act together. The retreat into isolation, which Brexit represents, not only damages Britain; it also significantly reduces the collective power of the EU to respond to the common difficulties faced by all Europeans, including the UK.

If we leave the EU with a deal, the 21-month transition period during which the UK remains a member of most EU arrangements, including the customs union and the single market, could provide the opportunity for a wide-ranging review of the impact of Brexit, covering not only trade and economics but also politics, security and international affairs. Indeed, whatever happens, including a no-deal outcome, it would make good sense to carry out such a review. The following are some of the issues which will need to be considered.

Sovereignty, power and influence

The Brexiteer slogan of "taking back control" is deeply flawed. It ignores the fact that, in or out of the EU, the freedom of a medium-sized state to act is seriously circumscribed. The late Lord Howe, former Tory Foreign Minister, pointed out that sovereignty is "not virginity, which you either have or you don't... rather it is a never-ending series of transactions between nation states, handing over some things and taking back others". He rightly argued for a modern, realistic approach to sovereignty, defined as a nation's practical capacity to maximise its influence in the world.

Thus Britain joined the EC to enhance its position, trading its formal sovereignty for a share in cooperative arrangements, which gave it a greater say. Belonging to the EC, and subsequently the EU, has provided Britain with the opportunity to participate in decisions that vitally affect us, assisting us to achieve, in cooperation with our partners, what Churchill called "that larger sovereignty".

Being a member of the EU has significantly increased the UK's power and influence. Having a 'seat at the table' of the EU, the world's largest market, has given the UK far greater clout than it would have had on its own. Recent history has shown that the EU has the size and capacity to negotiate with the world's biggest economies, such as the US, China, Japan and Canada, as well as the world's most powerful companies, including Amazon, Google, Facebook and Apple, in a way that would be impossible for the UK acting alone.

After Brexit, Britain will no longer be entitled to a seat at the EU's foreign affairs committee or on its political and security committee. Although the UK will remain a member of NATO, it will not be able to take part in the decision-making structure of EU common security and defence policy or joint EU missions at a time when these are gathering strength. Equally important is the loss of power, prestige and influence that the prospect of leaving the EU is already bringing about.

Defence and security

Writing in the *New Statesman*, Lord Kerr made a fundamental point about the value of international cooperation in today's fast-changing world and why Britain and other countries would be less secure after Brexit: "Most [EU leaders] believe that, in a world of Donald Trump and Vladimir Putin, of climate change and migration misery, Europe should stick together and work together."

It will, therefore, remain vital that the UK continues to cooperate on defence with its continental allies, not just through NATO, but also through European defence institutions. It is especially unfortunate that the UK intends to leave the EU just as the EU launches the Permanent Structured Cooperation (PESCO) which aims to coordinate joint missions more closely.

Furthermore, EU data sharing has proved extremely

valuable in fighting crime and preventing terrorist attacks. However, Barnier has stated that, after Brexit, the UK would be locked out of EU policing and security databases. He has also pointed out that the UK would lose access to the highly successful European arrest warrant scheme and would no longer have a role in key managing agencies such as Europol, the EU law enforcement agency, and Eurojust, the EU legal agency.

Growth, trade and employment

Being a member of the EU has transformed the UK from the 'sick man of Europe' to a prosperous economy. Between 1958, when the EEC was set up, and 1973, when Britain joined, gross domestic product (GDP) per head rose by 95 per cent in West Germany, France and Italy, compared with only 50 per cent in Britain. After becoming an EEC member, the UK began to catch up. And indeed, over the last 40 years, GDP per head has grown faster in the UK than in Germany, France and Italy. By 2013, Britain had become richer than the average of the three other large European economies.

The government's own leaked analysis (EU exit analysis January 2018) showed that the UK would suffer significant economic damage from all three main exit scenarios. In a no-deal scenario, under which Britain would rely on World Trade Organization rules alone, UK economic growth would be reduced by 8 percentage points over the next 15 years compared with current forecasts. Under a Canadian-style 'free-trade' agreement, growth would be 5 percentage points lower over the same period, while even the 'soft' Brexit option of retaining access to the EU single market through membership of the European Economic Area would reduce GDP by 2 percentage points. Under these three Brexit scenarios, almost every sector would be hit, with chemicals, clothing, manufacturing, food and drink, cars and retail suffering the most.

With Brexit, the enormous advantage that membership of the EU has brought to the British economy – above all through its membership of the customs union and the single market which gives it free access to its largest market (covering 44 per cent of the UK's total exports) – would be put at risk.

The CBI has also noted that the EU is a springboard for trade with the rest of the world, accounting for 23 per cent of the global economy in 2012 in dollar terms. Through 40 trade deals negotiated by the EU (and including the single market), British firms currently have full access to a $24 trillion market, a figure which will be greatly enhanced by recent trade deals with Canada and Japan.

The UK's membership of the EU has also made it by far the largest recipient of incoming foreign investment into the EU. Certainly, part of the UK's attractiveness for foreign investors is that it brings with it free access to the EU's single market. Brexit would put this flow of inward investment in danger. Indeed, it already has: in 2017, uncertainty about Brexit caused a 90 per cent drop in foreign direct investment (FDI) into the UK.

A June 2018 survey by the Swiss bank UBS found that one in three European firms plans to cut investment spending in the UK as a result of Brexit, and more than a tenth of those with operations in Britain expect to pull out of the country altogether. Inevitably, this will have unfavourable ramifications for jobs and employment in the UK, above all if we leave with no deal. Unfortunately, the impact is likely to be most damaging to the less prosperous parts of the UK, particularly the Midlands and the North of England, paradoxically those regions that voted most strongly to leave the EU.

The EU has been very successful in developing EU-wide scientific research programmes, of which the UK has been by far the largest beneficiary. More than 3 million European students have benefited from the EU's Erasmus programme since it was established in 1987. According to the British Council, 14,607 British students were working or studying in Europe through Erasmus in 2012/13, the highest level since the programme's launch. After Brexit, UK access to all these programmes would either have to be renegotiated or be put at risk.

Immigration, environmental protection and employees' rights

Free movement, which is one of the key principles of the EU, was a highly controversial issue during the 2016 referendum campaign, with misinformation and toxic propaganda from the Leave campaign helping to swing the vote in its favour. In fact, there are many advantages to migration from the EU. The fact that 82 per cent of working-age EU citizens in the UK are in employment – compared with 76 per cent of UK nationals and 63 per cent of people from outside the EU – demonstrate that migrants from the EU make up an integral part of our workforce. It is not always understood that, for many decades, non-EU immigration has been higher than immigration from the EU.

The contribution of EU citizens has been especially important to specific sectors of the economy, such as agriculture, hospitality and the auto industry. Above all, it is vital to our public services. The NHS, for example, is particularly reliant on EU migrants: 55,000 out of 1.2 million NHS staff members, including doctors, nurses, paramedics, pharmacists and support workers, are citizens of other EU countries. The pro-EU campaign group Open Britain has persuasively argued that the UK should be seeking to "mend not end" free movement, calling for an EU-wide examination of the working of free movement and looking at a range of reform options to mitigate any negative outcomes.

Environmental issues do not stop at national boundaries, so international agreements and cooperation are vital. EU legislation has been especially important for water, air quality, energy consumption and climate change, and has played a key role in protecting the environment in the UK. Under the Withdrawal Act, the Government is committed to transforming EU law into domestic law, but only where "practical" and "necessary".

Many rights for workers have been brought into UK law through EU membership, especially through the EU Social Chapter. Indeed, the TUC says that 41 out of 65 new health and safety regulations introduced between 1997 and 2009 came from EU laws. Following Brexit, some of these may be at risk.

Last Word

Theresa May and Boris Johnson argued that leaving the EU on the right terms could offer the UK a bright future, but there will clearly be big disadvantages. Being a member of the EU has brought great benefits to this country, including increased strength and power; more security and influence; faster expansion of trade, investment and employment; greater affluence and wellbeing; and improved environmental and social protection. Outside the EU, these advantages conferred by membership will no longer be available to us. To leave the EU would therefore be an act of self-inflicted folly.

In my view, it is likely that a review on the lines mentioned above will make plain that membership of the EU is essential for the future of the country. Speaking in the House of Lords on the second reading of the 14th January 2019 debate on the Withdrawal Agreement I predicted that, if we left the EU with a no-deal outcome or a half-hearted, botched arrangement, the outcome would be unacceptable to the next generation. Either result would not only make us poorer but separate us from our close continental neighbours who should be our natural partners. If I am right, and even if Brexit does go ahead, I predict that a new consensus will emerge in which there would be a large majority in favour of rejoining the EU on the conclusive and unanswerable grounds that a medium-sized power such as the UK should be acting together with its continental neighbours – not only for the good of its citizens, but for Europe as a whole.

If it is not possible to stop Brexit now, I believe the next generation will seek to rejoin the EU as soon as possible, returning to the organisation that has provided Britain and Europe with peace, stability and prosperity for over half a century.

HAUS CURIOSITIES

Inspired by the topical pamphlets of the interwar years, as well as by Einstein's advice to 'never lose a holy curiosity', the series presents short works of opinion and analysis by notable figures. Under the guidance of the series editor, Peter Hennessy, Haus Curiosities have been published since 2014.

Welcoming contributions from a diverse pool of authors, the series aims to reinstate the concise and incisive booklet as a powerful strand of politico-literary life, amplifying the voices of those who have something urgent to say about a topical theme.

'Nifty little essays – the thinking person's commuting read'
– *The Independent*

ALSO IN THIS SERIES

Britain in a Perilous World:
The Strategic Defence and Security Review We Need
by Jonathan Shaw

The UK's In-Out Referendum: EU Foreign and Defence Policy Reform
by David Owen

Establishment and Meritocracy
by Peter Hennessy

Greed: From Gordon Gekko to David Hume
by Stewart Sutherland

The Kingdom to Come: Thoughts on the Union
Before and After the Scottish Referendum
by Peter Hennessy

Commons and Lords: A Short Anthropology of Parliament
by Emma Crewe

The European Identity:
Historical and Cultural Realities We Cannot Deny
by Stephen Green

Breaking Point: The UK Referendum on the EU and its Aftermath
by Gary Gibbon

Brexit and the British: Who Are We Now?
by Stephen Green

These Islands: A Letter to Britain
by Ali M. Ansari

Lion and Lamb: A Portrait of British Moral Duality
By Mihir Bose

The Power of Politicians
by Tessa Jowell and Frances D'Souza

The Power of Civil Servants
by David Normington and Peter Hennessy

The Power of Judges
by David Neuberger and Peter Riddell

The Power of Journalists
by Nick Robinson, Barbara Speed, Charlie Beckett and Gary Gibbon

Drawing the Line: The Irish Border in British Politics
by Ivan Gibbons

Not for Patching: A Strategic Welfare Review
by Frank Field and Andrew Forsey

Fiction, Fact and Future: An Insight into EU Democracy
by James Elles